658.
409
z

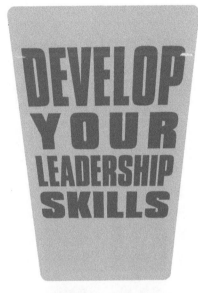

DEVELOP
YOUR
LEADERSHIP
SKILLS

CREATING SUCCESS

The best-selling series is back and better than ever

MARCH 2013

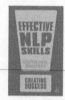

Because you only have one chance in life to make a good impression.

DEVELOP YOUR LEADERSHIP SKILLS

JOHN ADAIR

CREATING SUCCESS

KoganPage

First published in 2007 by Kogan Page Limited
Reissued 2010
Reprinted 2013 (twice), 2014 (three times)

2nd Floor, 45 Gee Street	1518 Walnut Street, Suite 1100	4737/23 Ansari Road
London EC1V 3RS	Philadelphia PA 19102	Daryaganj
United Kingdom	USA	New Delhi 110002
www.koganpage.com		India

© John Adair, 2007, 2010, 2013

The right of John Adair to be identified as the author of this work has been asserted by him in accordance with the Copyright, Designs and Patents Act 1988.

ISBN   978 0 7494 6700 5
E-ISBN   978 0 7494 6701 2

British Library Cataloguing-in-Publication Data

A CIP record for this book is available from the British Library.

Library of Congress Cataloging-in-Publication Data

Adair, John Eric, 1934-
    Develop your leadership skills / John Adair. – 2nd Edition.
        pages cm
    Includes index.
    ISBN 978-0-7494-6700-5 – ISBN 978-0-7494-6701-2   1. Leadership. I. Title.
    HD57.7.A2746 2013
    658.4′092–dc23   2012045516

Typeset by Graphicraft Limited, Hong Kong
Printed and bound by Ashford Colour Press Ltd.

CONTENTS

ABOUT THE AUTHOR

John Adair is the world's leading authority on leadership and leadership development. Over a million managers worldwide have taken part in the action-centred leadership programmes he pioneered.

John had a colourful early career. He served as a platoon commander in the Scots Guards in Egypt, and then became the only national serviceman to serve in the Arab Legion, where he became adjutant of the Bedouin regiment. He was virtually in command of the garrison of Jerusalem in the front line for six weeks. After national service he qualified as a deckhand in Hull and sailed an Arctic steam trawler to Iceland. He then worked as an orderly in the operating theatre of a hospital.

After being senior lecturer in military history and adviser in leadership training at the Royal Military Academy Sandhurst, and Associate Director of the Industrial Society, in 1979 John became the world's first Professor of Leadership Studies at the University of Surrey.

Between 1981 and 1986 John worked with Sir John Harvey-Jones at ICI, introducing a leadership development strategy that helped to change the loss-making, bureaucratic giant into the first British company to make £1 billion profit.

John has written over 40 books, translated into many languages. Recent titles include *How to Grow Leaders* and *Effective Leadership Development*. Apart from being an author, he is also a teacher and consultant.

From St Paul's School he won a scholarship to Cambridge University. John holds the higher degrees of Master of Letters from Oxford University and Doctor of Philosophy from King's College London, and he is also a Fellow of the Royal Historical Society. Recently the People's Republic of China awarded him the title of Honorary Professor in recognition of his 'outstanding research and contribution in the field of Leadership'.

INTRODUCTION

Leadership skills have now been universally recognized as a key ingredient – some would say *the* key ingredient – in management. A good manager is now by definition a leader. Equally, a *good* leader will also be a manager.

But how do you become such a leader? Is it possible to develop your own abilities as a leader? Let me answer that last question with a resounding YES. As for the first question, this whole book is my answer. It is a simple practical guide for anyone who is about to take up a team leadership role in any organization. But I hope that it will be equally useful for those already in such roles who wish to improve their basic leadership skills. If leadership matters to you, this book will give you a complete framework for becoming an effective leader.

One word of caution: nobody can teach you leadership. It is something you have to learn. You learn principally from experience. But experience or practice has to be illuminated by principles or ideas. It is when the sparks jump between the two that learning happens. So you will have to think hard, relating what I say to your experience as you read and reflecting on it. As with everything else in life, the more you put into this joint exploration of practical leadership, the more you will get out of it.

Let me add a bold claim for this short book. People often debate the differences and similarities of leadership and management. But the majority of practical people are interested primarily in what they have to do, and not whether it should be labelled 'leadership' or 'management' or both. As a Chinese proverb says,

'What does it matter if a cat is black or white, as long as it catches mice?' This is the book for such leaders. It is the first really successful synthesis of the concepts of leadership and management. At last there is a single integrated vision, a focus that encompasses both perspectives.

WHAT YOU HAVE TO BE

Let's start with the most basic question of all: why is it that one person rather than another emerges, or is accepted, as a leader within a group? In other words, what is leadership? The reason for starting here is that becoming clearer about the nature and role of leadership is the biggest step that you can take towards improving your own leadership skills. In the box below, give up to five responses to that question.

What is leadership?

1._____

2._____

3._____

4._____

5._____

One traditional answer to that question – which may be reflected in what you have written in the box – is that the person in mind has certain *leadership qualities*. These traits, such as courage or tenacity, tend to make people leaders in all circumstances. They are natural or born leaders.

There are two difficulties to this approach. First, if you compare all the lists of leadership qualities available in studies or books on the subject, you will notice considerable variations. That is not surprising, because there are over 17,000 words in the English language that describe personality and character. Secondly, the assumption that leaders are born and not made is not going to help you much. Remember that young person whose annual report stated that 'Smith is not a born leader yet!' Moreover, this assumption is not true. Naturally we do differ in terms of our potential for leadership, but potential can – and should – be developed. If you work really hard at leadership, your skills will become more habitual or unconscious. Then people will call *you* a natural leader.

SOME ESSENTIAL QUALITIES

You cannot leave personality and character out of leadership. There are some qualities that you have to have. Basically you should possess, exemplify and perhaps even personify the qualities *expected* or *required* in your working group. I have emphasized that because it is so fundamental. Without it you will lack credibility. (Incidentally, here is one of the first differences between leaders and managers: the latter can be appointed over others in a hierarchy regardless of whether or not they have the required qualities.)

These qualities are necessary for you to be a leader, but they are not in themselves sufficient to make you be seen as one. For example, you cannot be a military leader without physical courage. But there are plenty of soldiers with physical courage who are not leaders – it is a military virtue. So what other qualities do you need?

GENERIC LEADERSHIP TRAITS

You will have noticed that these qualities are very much anchored in particular fields. There may well be some commonality, but certainly the degrees to which the qualities are required will vary considerably. There are, however, some more generic or transferable leadership qualities that you should recognize in yourself – you will certainly see them in other leaders. They are set out in the box overleaf.

Qualities of leadership – across the board

- *Enthusiasm*. Can you think of any leader who lacks enthusiasm? It is very hard to do so, isn't it?

- *Integrity*. This is the quality that makes people trust you. And trust is essential in all human relationships – professional or private. 'Integrity' means both personal wholeness and adherence to values outside yourself – especially goodness and truth.

- *Toughness*. Leaders are often demanding people, uncomfortable to have around because their standards are high. They are resilient and tenacious. Leaders aim to be respected, but not necessarily popular.

- *Fairness*. Effective leaders treat individuals differently but equally. They do not have favourites. They are impartial in giving rewards and penalties for performance.

- *Warmth*. Cold fish do not make good leaders. Leadership involves your heart as well as your mind. Loving what you are doing and caring for people are equally essential.

- *Humility*. This is an odd quality, but characteristic of the very best leaders. The opposite to humility is arrogance. Who wants to work for an arrogant manager? The signs of a good leader are a willingness to listen and a lack of an overweening ego.

- *Confidence*. Confidence is essential. People will sense whether or not you have it. So developing self-confidence is always the preliminary to becoming a leader. But don't let it become overconfidence, the first station on the track leading to arrogance.

Some readers may question the inclusion of *integrity* in this list. Are there not good leaders, such as Adolf Hitler, who totally lacked integrity? There is a useful distinction between *good leaders* and *leaders for good*. Whether or not Hitler was a good leader is a debatable matter – in some respects he was and in others he was not – but he was certainly not a leader for good. But this is all a bit academic. For leadership that does not rest on the bedrock of integrity does not last: it always collapses, and usually sooner rather than later. Why? Because that is the way of human nature.

You can see that *what you are i*s an important strand in your leadership. Remember the Zulu proverb, 'I cannot hear what you are saying to me because you are shouting at me.' This strand in your leadership is also one of the three main paths up the mountain, the three lines of answering those core questions 'What is leadership?' and 'Why does one person rather than another emerge as the leader in a group?' (The other two approaches are considered in Chapters 2 and 3.)

Now, you can develop all these qualities. You can build your self-confidence, discover new wells of enthusiasm and grow in integrity. But it all takes time. It is better to start on one of the other two paths up the mountain. Although, having said that, I would counsel you to return to the qualities approach from time to time. Review your progress as the profile of your strengths and weaknesses (in terms of personality and character) begins to unfold and change in the positive direction. Always remain open to feedback on that score, however painful it may be (I speak from experience!).

In testing whether or not you have the basic qualities of leadership, you should ask yourself the questions in the following checklist.

CHECKLIST TO TEST QUALITIES

	Yes	No
Do I possess the above-mentioned seven qualities? (This 'test' will subsequently reveal whether or not you really do!)	☐	☐
Have I demonstrated that I am a responsible person?	☐	☐
Do I like the responsibility and the rewards of leadership?	☐	☐
Am I well known for my enthusiasm at work?	☐	☐
Have I ever been described as having integrity?	☐	☐
Can I show that people think of me as a warm person?	☐	☐
Am I an active and socially participative person?	☐	☐
Do I have the self-confidence to take criticism, indifference and/or unpopularity from others?	☐	☐
Can I control my emotions and moods or do I let them control me?	☐	☐
Have I been dishonest or less than straight with people who work for me over the past six months?	☐	☐
Am I very introvert or very extrovert (or am I an ambivert – mixture of both – as leaders should be)?	☐	☐

2

WHAT YOU HAVE TO KNOW

Another approach to leadership plays down the idea that there are such things as generic leadership qualities. It stresses the idea that leadership depends on the *situation*. In some situations one person may emerge as the leader; in others he or she may not. Winston Churchill, for example, was a great leader in wartime, but not so good in peace.

As we have seen, the truth is a little more complex than that. Some qualities are situation-related, but others – such as enthusiasm, moral courage and stamina – are found in leaders in widely different situations.

To my mind, the main contribution of this situational approach is that it emphasizes the importance of *knowledge* in working life; and knowledge is linked to *authority*. There are four forms of authority among people:

- *The authority of position and rank* – 'Do this because I am the boss!'

- *The authority of knowledge* – 'Authority flows to the one who knows.'

- *The authority of personality* – in its extreme form, charisma.

- *Moral authority* – personal authority to ask others to make sacrifices.

Nelson Mandela, for example, has dignity, integrity and charm. Because he endured years of imprisonment he has acquired the moral authority to ask his fellow countrymen and women to accept difficulties and hardships on the long road to national unity and prosperity.

Why do sailors do what the captain orders when the ship is tossed to and fro in a storm? Because they sense that the captain has the knowledge of the sea and navigation, deepened by experience of many other storms, to know what to do. Knowledge creates confidence in others.

For this reason your acquisition of technical and professional knowledge is actually part of your development as a leader. You are equipping yourself with one essential ingredient. To go back to Churchill for a moment, in 1940 he was the only cabinet minister with experience as a war minister in the First World War, quite apart from his own background as a professionally trained officer who, as a regimental commander, briefly served on the Western Front. Apart from his gifts of oratory and character, Churchill had a considerable amount of knowledge relevant to running a war – more so than his colleagues. And 'In the country of the blind, the one-eyed man is king'.

The same principle holds good for you. But don't imagine that having the appropriate technical or professional knowledge in itself qualifies you for leadership. Again, it is necessary but not sufficient.

All the main strands of authority – position, knowledge and personality – are important. In order to get free and equal people to cooperate and produce great results, you need to rely upon the second and third forms of authority as well as the first. It is like a three-stranded rope. Don't entrust all your weight to one strand only.

Martin is an outstanding technician, and he was pleased when he was promoted to team leader. The technical director in charge of production, Sally Henderson, had her doubts about Martin's abilities as a first-line manager, but promotion to a managerial role was the only way in that company of giving more money to people like Martin with long service and technical experience.

After some weeks the team's performance began to fall behind that of the others. Martin knew all the answers, but he did not listen. When things began to go wrong he became more of a bully. He reduced one team member to tears in front of the others.

'But I cannot understand it', Henderson said to the team while Martin was away for a few days recovering from stress. 'Isn't Martin a leader?'

'He certainly knows this factory backwards', replied one of the team. 'He is a real expert. But, no, we wouldn't use the word "leader" for him. He is no leader. There is more to leadership than technical knowledge.'

In the first phase of your career as a leader you will probably be working in a fairly well-defined field of work, and you will have acquired the necessary professional and technical knowledge. But, within your field, situations are changing all the time. How flexible are you? Can you cope, for example, with both growth and retraction? The following checklist will help you to confirm both that you are in the right field and also that you are developing the flexibility to stay in charge in a variety of different situations – including some that cannot be foreseen.

CHECKLIST: ARE YOU RIGHT FOR THE SITUATION?

	Yes	No
Do you feel that your interests, aptitudes (eg mechanical, verbal) and temperament are suited to the field you are in?	☐	☐
Can you identify a field where you would be more likely to emerge as a leader?	☐	☐
How have you developed 'the authority of knowledge'? Have you done all you can at this stage in your career to acquire the necessary professional or specialist training available?	☐	☐
Have you experience in more than one field or more than one industry or more than one function?	☐	☐

Do you take an interest in fields adjacent, and potentially relevant, to your own?

	Yes	No
Sometimes	☐	☐
Never	☐	☐
Always	☐	☐

How flexible are you within your field? Are you:

	Yes	No
Good – you have responded to situational changes with marked flexibility of approach; you read situations well, think about them and respond with the appropriate kind of leadership.	☐	☐
Adequate – you have proved yourself in some situations, but you fear others; you are happiest only when the situation is normal and predictable.	☐	☐
Weak – you are highly adapted to one particular work environment and cannot stand change; you are often called rigid or inflexible.	☐	☐

3

WHAT YOU NEED TO DO

A third line of thinking about leadership focuses on the group. This *group approach*, as it may be called, leads us to see leadership in terms of functions that meet group needs: what has to be done. In fact, if you look closely at matters involving leadership, there are always three elements or variables:

- *the leader* – qualities of personality and character;

- *the situation* – partly constant, partly varying;

- *the group* – the followers: their needs and values.

In fact, work groups are always different, just as individuals are. After coming together they soon develop a *group personality*, so that which works in one group may not work in another. All groups and organizations are unique.

But that is only half of the truth. The other half is that work groups – like individuals – have certain needs in common. There are three areas of overlapping needs that are centrally important, as illustrated in Figure 3.1.

Figure 3.1 Overlapping needs

TASK NEED

Work groups and organizations come into being because there is a task to be done that is too big for one person. You can climb a hill or small mountain by yourself, but you cannot climb Mount Everest on your own – you need a team for that.

Why call it a need? Because pressure builds up a head of steam to accomplish the common task. People can feel very frustrated if they are prevented from doing so.

TEAM MAINTENANCE NEED

This is not so easy to perceive as the task need; as with an iceberg, much of the life of any group lies below the surface. The distinction that the task need concerns things and the team maintenance need involves people does not help much.

Again, it is best to think of groups that are threatened from without by forces aimed at their disintegration or from within by disruptive people or ideas. We can then see how they give priority to maintaining themselves against these external or internal pressures, sometimes showing great ingenuity in the process. Many of the written or unwritten rules of the group are designed to promote this unity and to maintain cohesiveness at all costs. Those who rock the boat or infringe group standards and corporate balance may expect reactions varying from friendly indulgence to downright anger. Instinctively a common feeling exists that 'United we stand, divided we fall', that good relationships, desirable in themselves, are also an essential means towards the shared end. This need to create and promote group cohesiveness I have called the *team maintenance need*. After all, everyone knows what a team is.

INDIVIDUAL NEEDS

Thirdly, individuals bring into the group their own needs – not just the physical ones for food and shelter (which are largely catered for by the payment of wages these days) but also the psychological ones: recognition; a sense of doing something worthwhile; status; and the deeper needs to give to and receive from other people in a working situation. These individual needs are perhaps more profound than we sometimes realize.

They spring from the depths of our common life as human beings. They may attract us to, or repel us from, any given group. Underlying them all is the fact that people need one another not just to survive but to achieve and develop personality. This growth occurs in a whole range of social activities – friendship, marriage and neighbourhood – but inevitably work groups are extremely important because so many people spend so much of their waking time in them.

THE THREE CIRCLES INTERACT

Now these three areas of need overlap and influence one another. If the common task is achieved, for example, then that tends to build the team and to satisfy personal human needs in individuals. If there is a lack of cohesiveness in the team circle – a failure of team maintenance – then clearly performance in the task area will be impaired and the satisfaction of individual members reduced. Thus we can visualize the needs present in work groups as three overlapping circles, as shown in Figure 3.1.

Nowadays when I show the model on a slide or overhead I usually colour the circles red, blue and green, for light (not pigment) refracts into these three primary colours. It is a way of suggesting that the three circles form a universal model. In whatever field you are, at whatever level of leadership – team leader, operational leader or strategic leader – there are three things that you should always be thinking about: *task*, *team* and *individual*. Leadership is essentially an other-centred activity – not a self-centred one.

The three-circle model is simple but not simplistic or superficial. Keeping in mind those three primary colours, we can make an analogy with what is happening when we watch a television programme: the full-colour moving pictures are made up of dots of those three primary and (in the overlapping areas) three secondary colours. It is only when you stand well back from the complex moving and talking picture of life at work that you begin to see the underlying pattern of the three circles. Of course they are not always so balanced and clear as the model suggests, but they are nonetheless there.

TOWARDS THE FUNCTIONAL APPROACH TO LEADERSHIP

What has all this got to do with leadership? Simply this: in order to achieve the common task and to maintain teamwork, certain *functions* have to be performed. And a function is what you do, as opposed to a quality, which is an aspect of what you *are*. For example, someone has to define the objectives, make a plan, or hold the team together if it is threatened by disruptive forces.

Now we are on firm ground. For you can learn to provide the functions of leadership that are called for by task, team and individual needs. This is the entrance door to effective leadership. Moreover, you can – by practice, study, experience and reflection – learn to do the functions with skill: they will become your *leadership skills*. That does not mean that you will be performing all of them all of the time. But they will be like sharp, bright and well-oiled tools in your tool box, ready for instant use when need calls.

YOUR ROLE AS LEADER

You can now be crystal clear about your role as a leader. Let me explain the common but often misused word *role*. A metaphor drawn from the theatre, it points to the part assigned or assumed in the drama. In its wider social use, a role can be roughly defined as the *expectations* that people have of you. Of course, if different people have different expectations, you may experience *role conflict*. You may find, for example, that there is considerable tension at certain times in your life between the expectations of your parents, those of your life partner and those of your children.

We do not expect people to act outside their roles in the context of work. For instance, if a police officer stopped your car simply to tell you a joke that had been heard on television the previous night, most of us would – like Queen Victoria – not be amused. We do not expect police officers to behave in that way.

This is where the three-circle model comes in: what it does for you is to define the leader's role in a visual way. People *expect* their leaders to help them to achieve the common task, to build the synergy of teamwork and to respond to individuals and meet their needs. The overlapping circles integrate these three facets of the role.

Following the analogy of light, the leadership functions are like the spectrum of colours of the rainbow when a sunbeam is refracted through a prism (see Figure 3.2).

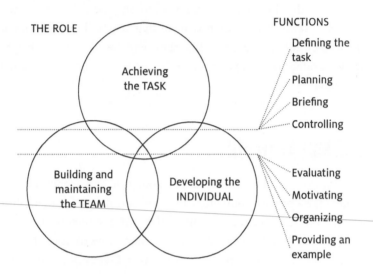

Figure 3.2 Leadership functions

In Chapter 4 we shall explore some practical ways in which you can perform these functions:

- at first with competence;

- after practice with skill;

- through self-development with excellence.

Here is your challenge as a leader or leader-to-be. Competence is within your grasp, but reach out for skill, and never rest content until you have achieved excellence in leadership.

LEADERSHIP: PERSONAL REMINDER

Whether in team, operational or organizational leadership, what matters is:

- *the leader* – qualities of personality and character;

- *the situation* – partly constant, partly varying;

- *the team* – the followers: their needs and values.

Three overlapping and interacting circles of needs, as shown in Figure 3.1, have to be focused on at all times. Leadership functions can be summarized as shown in Figure 3.2.

4

HOW TO TURN THE CORE LEADERSHIP FUNCTIONS INTO SKILLS

In this chapter I shall consider each of the main eight leadership functions in turn, and help you to identify ways in which you can perform them better.

Remember always that – because the three areas of task, team and individual overlap so much – any function will tend to affect all three circles. Take *planning*, for example. At first sight that appears to be solely a task function. Yet there is nothing like a bad plan to break up a team or frustrate an individual: it hits all three circles. Another general factor to bear in mind is that – as I have mentioned already – leadership exists on different levels:

- *team leadership:* you are leading a team of about 5 to 20 people;

- *operational leadership:* you are leading a significant unit in the business or organization, composed of a number of teams whose leaders report to you;

- *strategic leadership:* you are leading a whole business or organization, with overall accountability for the two levels of leadership below you.

Not only the three circles but the eight functions also apply at all these levels, although in different ways. In the brief discussions of each function below I shall sometimes indicate these differences, but my focus here is upon the first level – the team leadership role.

The functional approach to leadership set out here is also sometimes called *action-centred leadership*. A function is one of a group of related actions contributing to development or maintenance, just as each part of the body has its function in relation to the whole. 'Function' comes from a Latin word meaning *performance*. Sometimes it is used more widely to mean what I have called role – the special kind of activity proper to a professional position. Are you functional as a leader? In other words, are you capable of performing the regular functions expected of a leader?

DEFINING THE TASK

'Task' is a very general word. It simply means 'something that needs to be done', usually something that you are required to do. Generally speaking, people in teams or organizations have some idea of what they are there to do, but that general sense needs to be focused on to an *objective* that is:

- clear;

- concrete;

- time-limited;

- realistic;

- challenging;

- capable of evaluation.

By the last point I mean that there is a simple 'success criterion' that will enable you – and the team – to know that the objective has been achieved. If your target or goal is to reach the top of Mount Everest, for example, you will know when you attain it. In many other areas of human endeavour, of course, the success criteria are far less obvious.

Leadership is also about answering the question *why* as well as *what*. A boss may tell you *what* to do in a specific way, but a leader will explain or convey to you *why* as a first and important step on the road to your free and willing cooperation – the hallmark of all true leadership. There is an overlap here with motivation, or giving others a sufficient reason or grounds for action, which we shall discuss shortly. Here I want to stay within the task circle and suggest that all leaders should be able to relate an *objective* to the wider *aims* and *purpose* of the organization. In other words, they need to be able to think – and often to speak – in terms of a set of directions. When they do so they will be moving from the particular to the more general, from the concrete to the more abstract.

Gaia plc are in the business of profitably making and selling drilling equipment. You could call that their purpose, the reason they exist. They have three aims in their current strategy: to improve the quality of their best-selling range of oil and gas deep-sea drills, to capture 40 per cent of the world market over the next five years (at present they have 23 per cent) and to develop a range of new products for the gem-mining market, where high profits can be made.

> Mike Wilson is a team leader at their Aberdeen factory. The key objective for his team this week is to assemble a prototype drill to be part of the company's tender for business in the new oilfields off the Falkland Islands. By the end of the week the assembled drill has to be tested against five key quality criteria and a report written on the results. It has to be in the production director's hands by 6 pm on Friday.

If you were in Mike Wilson's shoes you could explain why the week's objective is important in terms of the company's aims. Equally, those aims have been identified and are being tackled *in order* to achieve the corporate purpose.

Coming the other way down Jacob's Ladder, you will be answering the question *how*. How are we in Gaia going to stay at the leading edge of profitably making and selling drilling equipment? Answer: by moving forward along the open-ended but directional paths indicated by our aims – improving quality, increasing market share and creating new products.

You will notice that Gaia are taking change by the hand before it takes them by the throat. Change is perhaps the most important factor that calls for leadership as opposed to mere management. Modern English *lead* is related to Old English words meaning 'a way, journey' and 'to travel'. It is a journey word. If you are not on a journey, don't bother with leadership – just settle for management.

CHECKLIST: DEFINING THE TASK

	Yes	No
Are you clear about the objectives of your group now and for the next few years/months, and have you agreed them with your boss?	☐	☐
Do you fully understand the wider aims and purpose of the organization?	☐	☐
Can you relate the objectives of your group to those larger, more general intentions?	☐	☐
Does your present main objective have sufficient specificity? Is it defined in terms of time? Is it as concrete or tangible as you can make it?	☐	☐
Will the group be able to know soon for themselves if you succeed or fail? Does it have swift feedback of results?	☐	☐

Hence leaders at all levels should stimulate and focus a sense of direction. 'Vision' literally means to see where you are going. Allied with some creative thinking, it can provide a new direction for a group or an organization. Change always brings the necessity to think very hard about your purpose, as well as your aims and objectives, in the context of the rapid changes in markets, technology, and economic and social life. That kind of thinking is the prime responsibility of strategic leaders, but if they are wise they will involve their operational and team leaders in this process as well. You need to understand the why behind the objectives you are being asked to achieve (see 'Checklist: defining the task').

PLANNING

Planning means building a mental bridge from where you are now to where you want to be when you have achieved the objective before you. The function of planning meets the group's need to accomplish its task by answering the question *how*. But the 'how' question soon leads to 'When does this or that have to happen?' and 'Who does what?'

From the leadership perspective, the key issue is how far you should make the plan yourself or how far you should share the planning function with your team. Again there is a distinction here between leadership and management, at least in its older form. F W Taylor, the founder of 'scientific management,' popularized the idea that things went better when there was a clear distinction between work on the one hand, such as making widgets, and the functions of planning and controlling on the other. The latter were the preserves of managers and supervisors. Do you agree?

There is a useful way of looking at the planning function as a cake that can be sliced in different proportions, as illustrated in Figure 4.1.

From the leadership angle the advantages of moving towards the right-hand side of the continuum in Figure 4.1 are considerable. The more that people share decisions affecting their working life, the more they are motivated to carry them out. That is one facet of what has been called 'empowerment'.

But, on the other hand, you will notice that when you work on the far right of the continuum you have lost control over the outcome. The team may make a plan that, although meeting the requirements you have identified, is not the way you would have done it yourself. Can you live with that?

Just where you should act on the planning continuum depends on several key factors, notably the time available to plan and the competence level of the team members. There is no one right 'style'. The best leaders are consistent – you know where you

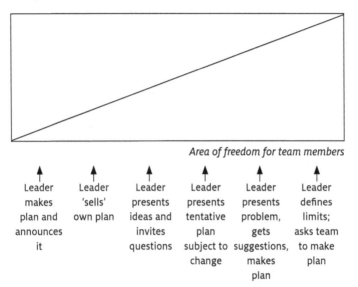

Use of authority by the leader

Area of freedom for team members

| Leader makes plan and announces it | Leader 'sells' own plan | Leader presents ideas and invites questions | Leader presents tentative plan subject to change | Leader presents problem, gets suggestions, makes plan | Leader defines limits; asks team to make plan |

Figure 4.1 The planning continuum

stand with them and they are in many respects predictable. But when it comes to decision making they are infinitely flexible. So a good leader, working with individuals or teams, will operate at different points on the scale during a day.

Once work has started on the plan, it may be necessary to revise or adapt the plan as circumstances or conditions dictate. Again, you must steer a middle course between the perennial need for flexibility as change unfolds and a certain persistence or tenacity in sticking to the agreed plan. Certainly, allowing too many unnecessary changes in the plan can in itself breed confusion. As the military proverb says, 'Order – counter-order – disorder.'

In summary, planning is a key activity for any team or organization. It requires a search for alternatives, and that is best done with others in an open-minded, encouraging and creative way. Foreseeable contingencies should always be planned for.

Planning requires that the what, why, when, how, where and who questions are answered. Plans should be tested...

CHECKLIST TO TEST PLANS

	Yes	No
Have I called upon specialist advice?	☐	☐
Have all feasible courses of action been considered and weighed up in terms of resources needed/available and outcomes?	☐	☐
Has a programme been established that will achieve the objective?	☐	☐
Is there a provision for contingencies?	☐	☐
Were more creative solutions searched as a basis for the plan?	☐	☐
Is the plan simple and as foolproof as possible, rather than complicated?	☐	☐
Does the plan include necessary preparation training of the team and its members?	☐	☐

BRIEFING

Briefing is the function of communicating objectives and plans to the team. It usually involves standing or sitting in front of the team and briefing them in a face-to-face way.

Like all functions, briefing can be done with skill, for there is a right way to brief a group and a wrong way. Briefing, in fact, is part of a much larger communication skill: effective speaking. Here are some guidelines:

- *Be prepared*. Rehearse and practise. Make sure that you have some professional-looking visual aids: 'A picture is worth a thousand words.'

- *Be clear*. Double-check that what you are saying is not vague, ambiguous or muddied – leave talk like that to the politicians!

- *Be simple*. Reduce complicated matter to its simplest form without oversimplifying. Avoid technical language or jargon that your audience will not understand.

- *Be vivid*. Colour your message with enthusiasm, confidence and humour. Make it live – make it exciting and challenging and fun.

- *Be natural*. You do not need to be a great orator. Just be yourself – your best self.

> Speak properly, and in as few words as you can, but always plainly; for the end of speech is not ostentation, but to be understood.
> WILLIAM PENN

Briefing is not something that you do only at the outset of a project and then forget about. Most probably, especially if the team is new or inexperienced, you will have to repeat the objective and plan as work progresses. It is always a function waiting to be performed.

Communication is the sister of leadership. Briefing points to only one skill, namely public speaking. Remember that listening is co-equal in importance. Everyone has something to contribute to the plan and its execution: ideas, suggestions or information. You need to be a listening leader.

Briefing sessions or conferences – work meetings – allow you to do some valuable work in all three circles, making general points connected with the specific matter in hand. In the task area, for example, you can make it the occasion for taking charge by giving direction and focus. A certain amount of assertiveness is often required of leaders, and the group will accept it – even welcome it – if the situation calls for it. You can stress the team approach to the task in hand, thus building up team spirit. You can meet *individual* needs by listening to and acknowledging the help of those who help you to achieve the ends of the meeting. It can also be an opportunity for emphasizing the significance of each individual's contribution to the success of the enterprise.

Team building: thoughts worth thinking

> You do not know me, I do not know you, but we have got to work together. Therefore, we must understand each other; we must have confidence in each other. I have only been here a few hours, but from what I have seen and heard since I arrived I am prepared to say here and now that I have confidence in you. We will work together as a team. I believe that one of the first duties is to create what I call atmosphere. I do not like the general atmosphere I find here – it is an atmosphere of doubt, of looking back. All that must cease. I want to impress upon everyone that the bad times are over and it will be done. If anybody here thinks it cannot be done, let him go at once. I do not want any doubters. It can be done and it will be done beyond any possibility of doubt.
>
> FIELD MARSHAL VISCOUNT MONTGOMERY, EXTRACT FROM SPEECH TO STAFF ON TAKING OVER THE EIGHTH ARMY, BEFORE THE BATTLE OF EL ALAMEIN

Some of the supreme examples of leadership occur when a leader takes over a demoralized group and 'turns it around'. The initial briefing meeting can be especially important in this process, for first impressions are as basic in working relationships as in love and friendship. The impression that you make on people at that first meeting will stay with them for ever. The task may have to be covered in general terms if you are new to the job – you can do little more than share your first thoughts. But you can share your vision, your spirit of resolve, and your determination to change the climate and standards of the group. That may require some tough talking, and people will wait to see if it is going to be backed up by equally firm deeds.

CONTROLLING

Controlling is the function of ensuring that all the energy of the team, and the resources at its disposal, are turning wheels and making things happen. Sometimes teams are like inefficient old steam engines, with much of their energies escaping like hissing steam into space and doing nothing to move the iron monster forward.

Of course humans are not machines, and some of their energy during the day will go into discussions or activities unrelated to the common task. Within reason, this 'time wasting' is acceptable, but it can become a problem in a team that does not have a really positive attitude to the common task.

Angela Roberts was appointed at a particularly difficult time as a team leader in a factory assembling television sets. Sales were falling, complaints about quality abounded, and morale was especially low. She noticed one symptom of this poor morale on her very first day in charge. The team members in the electronics factory where she had worked before usually took a 15-minute coffee break in the mornings, but here she found that 45 minutes was nearer the norm. 'You have a controlling problem', she told herself, and, being a good leader, by example and word she soon set a new standard.

It is the natural instinct of leaders (perhaps in contrast to managers) to rely as much as possible on self-control or self-discipline in others. The better the team and its constituent individual members, the more you can do that. The point about self-discipline is that it is our only way of being both disciplined or controlled *and* free. If control or discipline is imposed upon us – as sometimes it must be – we always lose an element of freedom. Now leadership only really exists among free and equal people, and so ultimately a large element of self-control is a necessary element of leadership. If a group or team, organization or community lack that, then they are also inadvertently robbing themselves of the opportunity to experience leadership as opposed to management.

'Control' comes from medieval Latin *contrarotulare* and originally meant 'to check accounts'. Its financial origin is a reminder that finance in different ways – profit targets and spending limits – is one important means of control. Self-managing teams (which are not the same as leaderless groups!) are those who take on board budget responsibility for planning and controlling their own work. Within limits they have discretion on how to use the resources – especially the money – that have been entrusted to them for achieving their agreed objectives.

Success at directing, regulating, restraining or encouraging individual and team efforts on the task (and in meetings) is the criterion for testing a leader's effectiveness as a 'controller'.

CHECKLIST FOR TESTING CONTROLLING SKILLS

	Yes	No
Do I maintain a balance between controlling too tightly and giving too much freedom to the team?	☐	☐
Am I able to coordinate work-in-progress, bringing together all the parts in proper relation to each other?	☐	☐

	Yes	No
In technical work, do I ensure that team and individual needs are met?	☐	☐
Do meetings I chair run over time(s) allotted to topics?	☐	☐
Do I have proper budgets and ways of monitoring actual performance?	☐	☐

Do customers rate my organization's control systems for:

	Yes	No
– quality of product/service	☐	☐
– delivery	☐	☐
– costs	☐	☐
– safety?	☐	☐

One essential strand in the concept of management, and one that is often overlooked in leadership, is relevant here. Management implies the efficient use of resources as well as their effective use. In these days of scarce resources – people's time, money and material in all its forms – the thrifty or economical use of resources is an imperative for all those who occupy organizational or community leadership roles. Good leaders will be managers in the sense that they husband carefully and spend to good effect the resources at their disposal. They get the maximum results with the minimum use of resources.

EVALUATING

As we have already seen, a key part of defining the task is establishing the *success criteria* – by which we shall know whether we are achieving the objective or at least making progress in its general direction. Evaluating, however, is much wider than that. It is that part of practical thinking that has to do with values.

Success has to do with values, ultimately with the values of the organization or the individual concerned. Performance has to be judged in relation to those values, which are usually implicit in the organization's purpose. It meets the task need circle, because people need to know where they are in relation to the end result they are aiming at.

Consequently, evaluating or review is not something that you, as a leader, leave to the 'wash-up' at the end. Whenever you comment on progress – or the lack of it – or invite the team to consider their own agreed success criteria, you are performing the function of evaluating.

Because it is a major mental function, an integral part of thinking (see my *Decision Making and Problem Solving* in the Creating Success series), valuing or evaluating will play a crucial role in your decision making. When you assess the possible consequences of a decision, for example, you will be evaluating. But you also evaluate in the other two circles: the team and the individual.

Why evaluate the team or get the team to evaluate its ways of working together? Because that is the principal way to *build* or develop the team. No team is perfect. Many are good; a few are very good; and still fewer are excellent. Here are some of the criteria or hallmarks of an excellent, high-performance team:

- *Clear realistic objectives.* Everyone knows what the team's objectives are and what their part in the plan is.

- *Shared sense of purpose.* By this I do not mean that every member can recite the organization's mission statement, but that you experience what engineers call a 'vector': direction plus energy.

- *Best use of resources.* All resources belong to the team and are put to work according to priority.

- *Atmosphere of openness.* There is excellent two-way communication between leader and members, and among members. People can speak openly, without fear of being thought critical. All that matters is to ensure that the best decisions are taken.

- *Handles failure.* Success is often to be found at the edge of failure. A high-performance team picks itself up quickly after a failure, learns the lessons and presses forward.

- *Rides out the storms.* The test of a high-performance team comes in the storms that overcome other, less stoutly made teams. The true evaluation of teamwork is in the difficult, demanding change situation.

When it comes to teamwork, remember that success often breeds failure. Successful teams sometimes become overconfident, even arrogant, and that is when they start making 'below the water-line' mistakes, the ones that can sink your organization. The price of excellence in teamwork is eternal vigilance.

As a leader, you should have a relationship with each member of the team – an equal but different relationship – as well as a relationship with the team as a whole. That will involve you in talking and listening to each individual. Your observations and conversations may lead you with some of them to take the role of a coach and counsellor.

If you work for an organization you may well have to *appraise* each team member. Appraising or evaluating individual performance is actually a natural expression of leadership. If it is formalized or systematized in your organization, you should take steps to avoid appraisal becoming a bureaucratic routine.

MOTIVATING

If communication is sister to leadership, then motivation is its brother. 'Motivation' comes from the Latin verb for 'to move'.

There is, of course, a variety of ways to move people: you can threaten them with punishments of one form or another, or induce them with financial rewards. Although motivating others in this way does fall within the compass of leadership as well as management, it is not characteristic of it.

I know that one of the things that leaders are supposed to do is to motivate people by a combination of rewards and sanctions. More recent thought suggests that we motivate ourselves to a large extent by responding to inner needs. As a leader you must understand these needs in individuals and how they operate, so that you can work with the grain of human nature and not against it.

In this field as in the others, it is useful for you to have a sketch map. Here A H Maslow's concept of a hierarchy of needs is still valuable (see Figure 4.2). He suggested that individual needs are arranged in an order of prepotence: the stronger at the bottom and the weaker (but more distinctively human) at the top.

The hierarchy of needs includes five categories:

- *Physiological* – our physical needs for food, shelter, warmth, sexual gratification and other bodily functions.

- *Safety* – the need to be free from physical danger and the need for physical, mental and emotional security.

- *Social* – the need for belonging and love, to feel part of a group or organization, and to belong or to be with someone else. Implicit in it is the need to give and receive love, to share and to be part of a family.

- *Esteem* – these needs fall into two closely related categories: self-esteem and the esteem of others. The first includes our need to respect ourselves, to feel personal worth, adequacy and competence. The second embraces our need for respect, praise, recognition and status in the eyes of others.

- *Self-actualization* – the need to achieve as much as possible and to develop one's gifts or potential to the full.

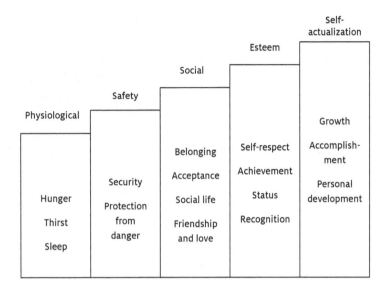

Physiological | Safety | Social | Esteem | Self-actualization

Hunger
Thirst
Sleep

Security
Protection from danger

Belonging
Acceptance
Social life
Friendship and love

Self-respect
Achievement
Status
Recognition

Growth
Accomplish-ment
Personal development

Figure 4.2 The hierarchy of needs

Maslow makes two interesting points. First, if one of our stronger needs is threatened, we jump down the steps of the hierarchy to defend it. You do not worry about status (see 'esteem'), for example, if you are starving (see 'physiological'). Therefore if you appear to threaten people's security by your proposed changes, then as a leader you should expect a stoutly defended response. Secondly, a satisfied need ceases to motivate. When one area of need is met, the people concerned become aware of another set of needs within them. These in turn now begin to motivate them.

There is obviously much in this theory. When the physiological and safety needs in particular have been satisfied they do not move us so strongly. How far this principle extends up the hierarchy is a matter for discussion.

Maslow's theory and other approaches based upon it are, I suggest, only a half-truth. Fifty per cent of our motivation comes from within us, as our unique pattern of individual needs unfolds inside ourselves and points us in certain directions. But the other 50 per cent comes from outside ourselves, and especially from the leadership that we encounter. I am not stating this 50:50 principle as a mathematical formula: it is just a way of saying that a very significant part of our motivation lies beyond us. Therefore as a leader you can have an immense effect upon the motivation of those around you. How do you do it? See 'Key principles for motivating others' below for some suggestions.

Inspiration is not quite the same as motivation. 'To inspire' means literally 'to breathe into' – 'inspiration' is a cousin of 'respiration'. Breath was once thought to be life – God's breath. So all inspiration was originally thought to be divine, and leadership itself – at least in its outstanding forms – was regarded as a divine gift.

What is it in a leader that inspires you? Enthusiasm, example, professional ability – there are many strands. But inspiration is found not only in the leader: the situation and the other people involved also contribute to a moment when hearts are lifted and spirits take on new life.

Have you ever reflected on how fortunate you are to have people working in your team who have these seeds of greatness in them? Your task is to locate, release and channel their greatness. It calls for all that is best in you.

Key principles for motivating others

- *Be motivated yourself.* If you are not fully committed and enthusiastic, how can you expect others to be?

- *Select people who are highly motivated.* It is not easy to motivate the unwilling. Choose those who have the seeds of high motivation within them.

- *Set realistic and challenging targets.* The better the team and its individual members, the more they will respond to objectives that stretch them, providing these are realistic.

- *Remember that progress motivates.* If you never give people feedback on how they are progressing, you will soon demotivate them.

- *Provide fair rewards.* Not easy. Do you reward the whole team, or each individual, or both? Either way, the perception of unfair rewards certainly works against motivation.

- *Give recognition.* This costs you nothing, but praise and recognition based upon performance are the oxygen of the human spirit.

ORGANIZING

Just as the language of leadership qualities is a bit imprecise – 'perseverance', 'tenacity' and 'stickability' mean, for instance, roughly the same thing – so the language of functions is also imprecise. Organizing is the function of arranging or forming into a coherent whole. It can mean systematic planning as well, but that is a function we have already covered. It encompasses the structuring – or restructuring – that has to be done if people are to work in harness as a team, with each element performing its proper part in an effective whole. You may, for example, break a larger group down into smaller subgroups.

At first sight you may think that the organizing function belongs more to the strategic and operational levels of leadership rather than to your role as a team leader. You are probably right as far as such factors as the size and structure of your group are concerned, or indeed its relations with other groups in the organization. But here I suggest that the organizing function concerns more than structuring or restructuring the architecture of organizations. If someone is described as a 'good organizer', what is meant by that phrase?

Much of the ground here has been covered already, such as being clear about the objectives, making a workable plan and structuring the group so as to facilitate two-way communication, teamwork and the appropriate measure of control. But there are three other aspects to be considered: systems, administration and time management.

Systems

Organizers tend to organize things by introducing systems. A 'system' is almost a synonym for an 'organization': a set of interrelated parts making up a whole. But 'system' can refer to *processes* – orderly or structured ways of doing things – as well as social structures.

Now you cannot run anything (even a fish and chip shop) without systems: production systems, selling systems, financial systems and so on. In large organizations there is a variety of other systems, such as an appraisal system or a quality control system.

A good leader understands the importance and value of systems. Almost by definition it is impossible to think of organizations that do not have systems or definite ways of doing things, although they are not always immediately apparent. Good leaders respect and work through the systems, changing them if need be. But they are not bound by them, like prisoners shackled in chains. They know when a system is becoming counterproductive.

Moreover, every system – if you think about it – requires teamwork to make it effective. So we come back to that core metafunction of leadership: building and maintaining the team. Have you noticed, too, that systems do not learn? Only people learn! Indeed, left to themselves systems are subject to one of the laws of thermodynamics: they run down and atrophy. To keep systems – the very essence of a corporate body – fit and healthy, good leadership at all levels is needed.

Administration

Administration is usually linked to management skills rather than leadership skills. You may be able to recall a leader you have met who was full of entrepreneurial spirit, enthusiasm and drive, a motivator of others but completely useless as an organizer and administrator. Indeed, 'industrial administration' was once the name for what we now call 'management'. The only relic of those days is the MBA – Master of Business Administration.

Administration, as we all know, involves paperwork and is primarily concerned with the day-to-day running of things. It usually includes financial administration of various kinds and levels.

Now the key thing to remember is that administration is always secondary to something else. It is a servant function. Minister is the Latin word for 'servant'; it comes from the familiar *minus*, 'less' (as opposed to the magister, '*master*', derived from *magis*, 'more').

In the old days, when organizations were overstaffed, you as the leader (alias *magister*) could delegate all the day-to-day paperwork to your staff. But these days leaders – equipped with personal computers – will often have to do a great deal more administration than in the past, especially at team leader level. So being a good administrator is now a part of being a good leader.

Taking on this administrative responsibility of leadership is a way of becoming a good facilitator, for you are thereby freeing the team as a whole and its individual members to be effective, creative and innovative. That does not mean to say that you should do all the administration – far from it. You need to delegate so that you have time to think and time to lead. But you should perform the administration that cannot be delegated (either because of its nature or because you lack anyone to delegate it to) in such a way that you are providing a good example. If you are late and sloppy doing the paperwork in returns, how can you expect others to be on time with their returns? Make sure that your team has a reputation for excellence in all administrative matters.

Lastly, seeing yourself in part as an administrator helps to create real teamwork in the organization. For you will come to appreciate more and more the contributions of those in the 'back room' of the enterprise, those who are primarily administrators. Their work may be more mundane and more behind-the-scenes, but it is vital to the success of the organization as a whole and to your team in particular. Remember to share your success with these invisible members of your team!

Time management

Leaders need time to think, time for people – customers as well as team members – and time to grow the business. Therefore they should be skilled managers of their own time. If you cannot organize yourself, how can you organize anyone or anything else? Administering that scarce resource, your own time, is the priority for any leader.

EXERCISE

Keep a log of how you spend your time over a two-week period, if possible charting every half-hour at work. Then go through it putting a 'T' for 'Task', 'TM' for 'Team Maintenance', and 'I' for 'Individual Needs' beside each item. You may of course put more than one of these code letters beside each item.

This exercise, properly done, will give you an idea of how much of your key resource – time – is not being spent in your core role as a leader.

Now ask yourself, 'What am I being paid to do?'

Time management is made up of applying some underlying principles – know your purpose, aims and objectives, for example – and some practical policies and tips. Learning to say no, which sounds so simple, can save you a bundle of time.

CHECKLIST FOR TESTING YOUR ORGANIZING FUNCTION ABILITY

	Yes	No
Can you organize your personal and business life in ways that would improve your effectiveness as a leader?	☐	☐
Can you delegate sufficiently?	☐	☐
Can you identify improvements in your time management?	☐	☐

Team

	Yes	No
Is the size and make-up correct?	☐	☐
Should a sub-team be set up?	☐	☐
Are opportunities and procedures in place to ensure participation in decision making?	☐	☐
Do you restructure and change individuals' jobs as appropriate?	☐	☐

Organization

	Yes	No
Do you have a clear idea of its purpose and how the parts should work together to achieve it?	☐	☐
Are effective systems in place for training, recruitment and dismissal?	☐	☐

	Yes	No
Do you carry out surveys into the size of teams, number of leadership levels, growth of unnecessary complexity, line and staff cooperation and properly working communications systems?	☐	☐
Are you good at administration, recognizing the performance of administrators and ensuring that administrative systems facilitate excellent performance from teams and individuals?	☐	☐

PROVIDING AN EXAMPLE

'Leadership is example,' someone once said to me. Certainly it is impossible to think of leadership without example. It may take many shapes and forms, but it has to be there.

In the context of communication, you can think of example as a prime means of communicating a message through 'body language' or non-verbal communication. Or, as the modern management proverb puts it, you have to 'walk the talk'.

A short course on leadership

The six most important words...
'I admit I made a mistake.'

The five most important words...
'I am proud of you.'

The four most important words...
'What is your opinion?'

The three most important words...
'If you please.'

The two most important words...
'Thank you.'

The one most important word...
'We.'

And the last, least important, word...
'I.'

Remember that you cannot avoid being an example of some kind or other, simply because the people who work with you will always observe what you are and what you do as well as what you say. 'A manager will take six months to get to know his staff,' goes a Japanese maxim, 'but they will take only six days to get to know him.' Example, in other words, is just you. But you do have some discretion as to whether it will be a good or poor example.

EXERCISE

Look back over your career and see if you can identify two people who have been astounding examples of good and bad leadership. List on paper the non-verbal ways in which these examples were expressed. What, in each case, were the effects on you? Did others notice their example? What effects did their example have on the group or organization?

As a general principle, we notice bad example more than good. It shouts at us more. It is always a pleasure to see good example, however, even if others seem impervious to it. It is always a sign of integrity: that wholeness that binds together what you say with what you do. A hypocrite – one who publicly preaches one thing and acts quite differently in private life – is neither setting an example nor expressing integrity. 'Do not, as some ungracious pastors do,' wrote Shakespeare, 'show me the steep and thorny way to heaven, whilst... himself the primrose path of dalliance treads.' There you have it.

'Pastor' means 'shepherd'. In ancient times the role of the shepherd was a model for leadership. For the shepherd had to lead his flock – or hers, because women as well as men herded sheep – on a journey to pasture (task), hold it together as a unity when wolves threatened (team maintenance) and care for each sheep (individual needs). The word 'good' in the New Testament phrase 'I am the good shepherd' means in the original Greek 'skilled' or 'competent', not 'good' in the moral sense.

CHECKLIST TO TEST IF YOU SET A GOOD EXAMPLE

	Yes	No
Do you ask others to do what you would be unwilling to do yourself?	☐	☐
Do people comment on the good example you set in your work?	☐	☐
Does your (bad) example conflict with what all are trying to do?	☐	☐
Can you quote when you last deliberately set out to give a lead by example?	☐	☐
Can you think of ways you could lead by example?	☐	☐
Do you mention the importance of example to team leaders who report to you?	☐	☐

Now, as I have already mentioned, there is a distinction between 'good leadership' and being a 'leader for good', although it is not one I would want to press too far. You should set yourself the ideal of being both. For only 'leadership for good' works with human nature *in the long run*.

What is a *good* example? Again, the three-circle model can help us. Look at 'Key questions for good leadership' in the box below.

One very powerful form of leading by example is sharing fully in the dangers, hardships and privations experienced by the team. What do you think of the chief executive and board of directors of an ailing, publicly quoted company who voted themselves a 60 per cent pay rise while downsizing the work-force and insisting that the remaining staff accepted only 2 per cent (less than the rate of inflation)?

Key questions for good leadership

- *Task*. The core action of going out in front on the journey in order to show the way is a form of leading by example. How can you 'lead from the front' in your field?

- *Team*. As a builder and maintainer of the team you need to maintain or change group standards – the invisible rules that hold groups together. How can you develop your team's standards through the power of example?

- *Individual*. Think of each team member as a leader in his or her own right. Each should be a leader in his or her technical or professional role, and a 'three-circle' contributor.

You can see now the importance of this function of providing an example, but can it be done with skill? At first sight, no, for skill implies a conscious learning of an art. To set an example consciously in order to influence others seems to be rather manipulative. That is why I talk about *providing* an example, rather than *setting* one. For you can provide an example in an unselfconscious way, as an expression of who you are as opposed to something done for a carefully calculated effect. If example becomes a habit, you will not think about it – still less congratulate yourself on being such a good leader!

It follows that if you are going to lead effectively by example as much as by other means you will need at least modesty if not humility – that rarest of all qualities in leadership, found only in the best. The Chinese philosopher Lao Tzu summed it up in the sixth century before the Christian era:

A leader is best

When people barely know that he exists;

Not so good when people obey and acclaim him;

Worst when they despise him.

Fail to honour people,

They fail to honour you.

But of a good leader, who talks little,

When his work is done, his aim fulfilled,

They will all say, 'We did this ourselves.'

Yes, and perhaps one day they will add about you as their leader, 'And *you* made a difference.' That is the true reward of leadership.

HOW TO DEVELOP YOURSELF AS A LEADER

Much of my professional life has been spent in trying to persuade organizations of all sizes to grow their own leaders. In that work, as I once heard a US bishop say, I have had enough success to prevent me from despair and enough failure to keep me humble. But from experience and observation I have to tell you that most good leaders emerge and grow *in spite* of their organizations rather than *because of* them. Moreover, you will most probably work for five or six organizations in your career, so none of them will be quite as committed to your long-term development as you are. How then do you develop yourself as a leader?

There is no infallible system or set of systems, I am afraid. You are a unique person, with a unique path of leadership in front of you. Nobody can teach you the way: you have to find it for yourself. If it was an easy path, a lot more people in leadership roles or positions would be showing the skills of leadership as outlined in these pages than is actually the case.

All I can do is share with you some practical suggestions and reflections that you may find useful. I hope that you will find them encouraging in nature, because on a journey we all need inspiration (even to write books!). As the eighteenth-century poet John Collier truly said, 'Not geniuses, but average men and women require profound stimulation, incentive towards creative effort and the nurture of great hopes.'

BE PREPARED

The door into leadership has 'Confidence' written upon it. You have to *want* to be a leader. It begins with a willingness to take charge. If you hate the idea of taking responsibility for the three circles, then leadership is not for you. Remain an individual contributor. 'You cannot put into yourself what God has not put there', as a Hungarian proverb says.

Given you fulfil that basic requirement of a willingness to accept responsibility, never write yourself off as a potential leader. It is a question of getting yourself into the right field and then waiting for the right situation. But remember Louis Pasteur's famous remark that 'Fortune favours the prepared mind'. The more prepared you are, the more confident you become. Remember as a leader or leader-to-be always to look confident, even when you may not be feeling it inside. People will tend to take you at face value.

BE PROACTIVE

Organizations do have a vested interest in your development as a leader, because they *need* leaders. Share with them your hopes, intentions and ambitions. You should be seeking above all opportunities to lead, be it leadership of a team or a project group. Experience is a compost heap of successes and failures. Make compost! Without it you can hardly grow as a leader.

Apart from promotion to a leadership role, organizations may well offer you – perhaps in response to a request from yourself – some leadership training. It may be either an internal or an external course. Seize these opportunities with both hands. You will be able to practise your skills and receive useful feedback. You should, of course, remain constructively critical, for not everything you hear on leadership courses or read in books is both true and practicable. But it is a key opportunity for stimulation and learning. Take any such offers.

BE REFLECTIVE

Most leaders are action-centred and fairly well immersed in their work, not least because they tend to love it. You do need, of course, to be able to withdraw from time to time and take a 'helicopter view' of what is going on. These times of reflection should include your own role performance as a leader. List the things that are going well and identify some specific areas for self-improvement. This process is a natural one in any aspect of our lives – as husbands, wives or partners, for example – but you should upgrade it into a self-learning method. It will yield you a mental list of action points aimed at improving your skills and knowledge as a leader.

Using informal or unstructured feedback is an especially important self-development tool. People are rather like mirrors or 'social reflectors': they beam back to us how we are coming across.

In this respect, however, others are imperfect receptors or mirrors, for they do not merely observe you: they also interpret what they see before giving you their feedback – solicited or unsolicited. So you do have to be cautious in using feedback. You may have to unpack the observation from the interpretation. Remember that you are only receiving others' impressions, not true psychological statements about the inner you. Always look for a pattern. As the proverb says:

If one person says that you are a horse,
Smile at them.

If two people say that you are a horse,
Give it some thought.

If three people say that you are a horse,
Go out and buy a saddle.

Feedback is a bit like the guidance mechanism in a rocket. If you receive it with an open mind, looking for the truth in it, it can guide you on your path to excellence in leadership.

Never be afraid of failure. The path forward will be strewn with the results of your failures as a leader. For the only way you can move from being a good leader – where you are now – to becoming a very good leader, even an excellent or a great one, is by aiming higher. And that is bound to generate short-falls. But persevere. In the end they may say of you that you are a born leader!

Developing your basic confidence using the well-tested frameworks set out in this book, enlisting the help of your organization as a partner in your leadership development, and making discriminating use of the feedback coming your way from all sources – superiors, colleagues, team members, friends and family – are but three practical ways in which you can improve your leadership. You can doubtless think of others. It does take time, for there is no such thing as instant leadership. Therefore be patient with yourself. Aim to take a step forward each day. Do something differently tomorrow as a result of reading this book. However small a step it is, you will be on your way. Read this book again at regular intervals: it will help you to keep moving forward. For, as a true leader, like Wordsworth's 'Happy Warrior', you should be one who

Looks forward, persevering to the last,
From well to better, daily self-surpassed.

HOW TO LEAD AT
THE STRATEGIC LEVEL

It is better to have a lion at the head of an army of sheep
than a sheep at the head of an army of lions.
DANIEL DEFOE

Earlier in this book I mentioned that leadership takes place on
three broad levels: team, operational and strategic. The essential
nature of leadership as response to the three circles – task, team
and individual – remains unchanged at all these levels. What
changes is complexity. As compared to the team leader's role, the
task of the strategic leader is both longer-term and more complex.
The team that he or she has to harmonize and align on to the
common purpose may be extremely large, subdivided into many
units and geographically disperse.

THE FUNCTIONS OF A STRATEGIC LEADER

'Strategic leadership', a phrase that I coined in the 1970s for the work of the leader of an organization, is an expansion of *strategy*. In ancient Greek, *strategy* is composed of two words: *stratos*, a large body of people such as an army in camp, and *egy*, leader (the English word *hegemony*, leadership among nations, derives from it). So strategy in our modern sense – as contrasted with tactics – is only one small segment of what the Greeks meant by the word. For them it encompassed the whole art of being a commander-in-chief, including principally what we call leadership.

You need to prepare yourself for strategic leadership as thoroughly as you can – this chapter may give you some clues as to the path you should take. Never let it be said of you what the Roman historian Tacitus once wrote of Emperor Galba: 'No one would have doubted his ability to reign had he never been emperor.'

What fits a person to fulfil this role? It is clearly a demanding and challenging one, even though there are professional staff at hand – sometimes in cohorts – to help the strategic leader where the responsibilities are great.

You will need awareness, understanding and skill in the three-circle model. A thorough knowledge of your business is essential. Personal qualities mentioned already, such as enthusiasm, integrity, fairness, toughness, calmness, humanity, resilience and a measure of humility, are also important. You also need to be able to think clearly and reason cogently.

Table 6.1 The key functions of strategic leadership

FUNCTION	AREA OF RESPONSIBILITY
Providing direction for the organization as a whole	Purpose, vision
Getting strategy and policy right	Strategic thinking and planning
Making it happen (overall executive responsibility)	Operational/administration
Organizing or reorganizing (balance of whole and parts)	Organization fitness to situational requirement
Releasing the corporate spirit	Energy, morale, confidence, esprit de corps
Relating the organization to other organizations and society as a whole	Allies, partners, stakeholders, political, society
Choosing today's leaders and developing tomorrow's leaders	Teaching and leading by example – a learning culture

THE IMPORTANCE OF PRACTICAL WISDOM

'It is easy to find a thousand soldiers but very difficult to find a general', says the Chinese proverb. One reason is that the combination of the necessary intellect with proven inspirational ability as a leader is very rare. I don't mean academic scholarship or what is commonly called being clever. 'Too much intellect is not necessary in war', Napoleon once wrote in a letter to his brother Joseph. 'Probably the most desirable attribute of all is that a man's judgement should be above the common level. Success in war is based on prudence, good conduct and experience.'

The Greeks, of course, had a word for it. The essential quality they looked for in a strategic leader – essential for leading one's personal life too – was *phronesis*. Translated into Latin as *prudentia* and thus into English as *prudence*, it really means practical wisdom. You may like to reflect upon my suggestion that practical wisdom is composed of three principal ingredients: intelligence, experience and goodness. That is why we call Gandhi or Nelson Mandela wise, but not Hitler, Stalin or Saddam Hussein.

A key point to remember about strategic leadership is that in all but the smallest organizations the role is too big for one person to do it all him- or herself. You have to be able to delegate effectively, leaving yourself time to think and time for people. You may even share the role (as a chairman and chief executive do). Be that as it may, you will certainly need to build a strategic leadership team around you – including the senior operational heads – to ensure that you meet the challenges of the three circles in these turbulent times of change.

EXERCISE

Sir Terry Leahy, chief executive of Tesco, believes that the essence of his job is leadership. 'There is a simple recipe for leadership,' he told me, 'which is to find out the truth of the situation, paint a picture of where you want to get to, make a plan and go and do it. It applies to businesses and cities but it also applies to your own personal situation. Always believe that there is a better place and then persuade people to go there with you.'

Of the seven functions of a strategic leader (see Table 6.1), which are the ones that Terry Leahy highlights for us?

LEADERSHIP FOR DESIRABLE CHANGE

Change and leadership are closely linked. Change throws up the need for leaders; leaders bring about change. As the proverb says, 'The bird carries the wings and the wings carry the bird.' You can manage the *effects* of change maybe, but positive, desirable change always calls for leadership.

That principle, incidentally, not only applies to your organization as you navigate its path forward on the turbulent seas of change. It is true, too, of society at large. Democracy always calls for good leaders – and leaders for good. 'Men and women make history', President Harry S Truman said, 'and not the other way round. *In periods where there is no leadership society stands still.* Progress occurs when courageous, skilful leaders seize the opportunity to change things for the better.'

> Your position never gives you the right to command. It only
> imposes on you the duty of so living your life that others
> can receive your orders without being humiliated.
>
> DAG HAMMARSKJOLD

HOW TO GROW LEADERS IN YOUR ORGANIZATION

When you are young, or at least upon the early rungs of your career, you are understandably focused upon developing to the full your own potential as a leader, but once you are in a leadership role at team level you have a responsibility for developing the individuals in your team (the third circle), and that includes their abilities as leaders. At the strategic level, so important is this work of fostering effective leaders for today's performance and tomorrow's growth that it constitutes one of the seven core functions that together make up the role. How do you do it?

PRINCIPLE ONE: DEVELOP A STRATEGY FOR LEADERSHIP DEVELOPMENT

The key to achieving sustainable business success is to have excellence in leadership at all three levels. Strategic, operational and team leaders need to work harmoniously together as the organization's leadership team.

The most common and most expensive error that organizations are committing at present is to focus leadership development on their more senior managers, so that becomes their entire 'strategy'. In so doing, they completely ignore their team leaders. Yet it is the team leader who is closest to the customer. Make sure that your strategy embraces all three levels.

There is a useful distinction to be made between strategic thinking and strategic planning. You should see your leadership development strategy – evolved and guided by a small steering group – as part of your overall business strategy. It should be longer-term (5 to 10 years). Don't let the urgent deflect you from the important, for a strategy worth the name should be three-dimensional:

- *importance* – it really has to matter;

- *longer-term* – it takes time to grow trees;

- *multi-factored* – it takes more than one element or approach to make a strategy.

The remaining principles will give you an idea of what those various elements should be. It is when there is synergy – the key elements working together in harmony – that your organization will begin to grow leaders.

PRINCIPLE TWO: SELECTION

'Smith is not a born leader yet.' When those words appeared on a manager's report in the 1950s, nobody thought that the person in question could do anything about it – still less the organization that employed him. As a saying of the day had it, 'Leaders are born and not made.'

We don't think like that now. The action-centred leadership course based on the three-circle model that was developed in the 1960s proved once and for all that the proverb was only half-true – leaders can be trained or developed. The other half of the truth, however, is that people do vary in their relative amount of leadership potential. Since it is not easy to develop leaders, why not hire people who are halfway – or more – there already? Or at least make sure that when you recruit from outside – or promote from inside – you know how to select those with a high potential for becoming effective leaders, for it is leaders who will grow your business rather than just administering it.

Remember that a *person* can be appointed a *manager* at any level, but he or she is not a leader until the appointment has been ratified in the hearts and minds of those who work with the person. If too few managers in your organization are receiving that kind of accolade, who is to blame? Not the manager in question, I suggest, but those who failed to apply principle two when they appointed the person in question. You cannot teach a crab to walk straight.

PRINCIPLE THREE: TRAINING FOR LEADERSHIP

To *train* implies instruction with a specific end in view; *educate* implies attempting to bring out latent capabilities. Of course, there is no hard-and-fast line between training and education. Think of it more as a spectrum of combinations between the two poles. For brevity's sake, I shall refer here to both as training.

As part of your strategic thinking, you should identify your business training needs in the leadership context and assign them priorities. Bear in mind always that training of any kind is going to cost your organization time and money. You need courses or programmes that are effective – they produce good leadership – and also cost-effective (in terms of time and money). If you have large numbers (like the NHS), you need high-volume, high-quality and low-cost courses.

The first level to look at is your team leaders, alias first-line managers. Do newly appointed team leaders have training in leadership prior to or shortly after appointment? In my view, it is actually morally wrong to give a person a leadership role without some form of training – wrong for the person and wrong for those who work with the person. We do not entrust our children to bus drivers who have no training, so why place employees under the direction of untrained leaders?

If you outsource your in-company leadership training to external providers, make sure that you retain 'ownership' and control, so that the programmes fit in with your strategy and organizational ethos. Delegation never means abdication.

PRINCIPLE FOUR: CAREER DEVELOPMENT

People grow as leaders by the actual practice of leading. There is no substitute for experience. What organizations almost uniquely can do is to give people opportunities to lead. The trick here is to give a person the right job at the right time. It should be the kind of leadership role that is realistic but challenging for the individual concerned. No stretch, no growth.

If your organization is serious about applying this principle, it will, for example, have a conversation once a year with each leader or would-be leader in which it outlines what it has in mind for the individual concerned. Equally, such a meeting is an opportunity for the individual to be proactive and to say what he or she aspires to do. The individual may, for example, want to move out of a specialist role to a more generalist (leadership) one. Fitting together this jigsaw of hopes and expectations is the name of the game, and it should be a win-win situation. A strategic leader in the making – possibly as your successor – will need experience in more than one functional area of the business and, if you are an international company, in more than one country.

PRINCIPLE FIVE: LINE MANAGERS AS LEADERSHIP DEVELOPERS

In the midst of the Battle of El Alamein in 1942, Montgomery found time to telephone General Horrocks, one of his top operational leaders and a newly appointed corps commander, and give him a tutorial on leading at that level. For Monty had observed that Horrocks had been reverting to being a divisional general. All good leaders are also teachers.

A leader's responsibility for individual needs – that third area of need – includes developing the individual's potential – both professional and technical and in the 'human side of enterprise'. That entails one-to-one meetings at regular intervals to offer constructive criticism, as well as encouragement or support.

Above team level (and some would say even at team level) all leaders are 'leaders of leaders', as was said about Alexander the Great. Good leaders will use their one-to-one opportunities – formal or informal – to share their knowledge of leadership in a conversational but effective way. It is, if you like, the apprentice approach to learning leadership, and its necessary condition is mutual respect. It is that mutual trust or respect that makes us both eager to learn and ready to teach. You need a system of setting objectives and appraising performance – part of action-centred leadership – but it won't be complete unless it is seen as a channel for two-way learning.

PRINCIPLE SIX: CULTURE

Wellington and Nelson, Slim and Montgomery – yes, the armed services do grow leaders. They select and train for leadership, but their real secret is that since the 18th century they place a high value on leadership. They have a culture where it is valued at all levels. Above all, it is expected from all officers. The motto of Sandhurst expresses the ideal that is expected from every officer: *Serve to Lead*.

Values are the stars your organization steers by and together they define your distinctive ethos. Make sure your culture comes to place a high value on 'good leadership and leadership for good'. In the final analysis, it is culture that grows leaders, so it is vital to review it and make changes where necessary.

Corporate culture should also encourage a climate of self-development in leadership. Organizations only have 50 per cent of the cards in their hands; the other 50 per cent are in the hands of the individual. There may be no leadership courses available to you, but you can still learn leadership. Books are the best method, together with reflection on your own experience.

Perhaps your organization needs a motto too. How about the Latin motto of the United Kingdom's Chartered Institute of Management, *Ducere est Servire* – To Lead is To Serve?

PRINCIPLE SEVEN: THE CHIEF EXECUTIVE

The seven generic functions of a strategic leader make it crystal clear that if you are in the role of chief executive you own the problem of growing leaders. Human resources or training specialists are there to advise and help. They can assist you to formulate and implement your strategy, but you are in the driving seat. If not, don't expect any forward movement.

Apart from taking responsibility for the strategy, you should also be leading it from the front yourself. Be known to talk about leadership on occasion – not often but sometimes and always effectively. Visit any internal leadership courses and show your support for them. If you care about leadership, so will the organization. Incidentally, it is also a chance to get your message across, as well as an opportunity to practise the skill of listening. Organizations today need listening leaders.

FINDING GREATNESS IN PEOPLE

In conclusion, developing future leaders is not a mystery. We know the laws of aerodynamics that undergird successful and sustained leadership development. The seven principles identified in this chapter are the foundations you are looking for, but it is up to you to apply them in the context of your organization's needs and requirements.

So it is going to take you some time, effort and money. Why bother? The answer is simple. The tasks that face us are ever more challenging. In order to respond to them, people at all levels need effective and inspiring leaders.

As John Buchan said, 'The task of leadership is not to put greatness into people but to elicit it, for the greatness is there already.'

APPENDIX
A LEADERSHIP CHECKLIST

ACHIEVING THE TASK

- *Purpose.* Am I clear what my task is?

- *Responsibilities.* Am I clear what my responsibilities are?

- *Objectives.* Have I agreed objectives with my superior?

- *Working conditions.* Are these right for the group?

- *Resources.* Are there adequate authority, money and materials?

- *Targets.* Has each member clearly defined and agreed targets?

- *Authority.* Is the line of authority clear?

- *Training.* Are there any gaps in the specialist skills or abilities of individuals in the group required for the task?

- *Priorities.* Have I planned the time?

- *Progress.* Do I check regularly and evaluate?

- *Supervision.* In case of my absence, who covers for me?

- *Example.* Do I set standards by my behaviour?

BUILDING AND MAINTAINING THE TEAM

- *Objectives*. Does the team clearly understand and accept them?

- *Standards*. Do they know what standards of performance are expected?

- *Safety standards*. Do they know the consequences of infringement?

- *Size of team*. Is the size correct?

- *Team members*. Are the right people working together? Is there a need for subgroups?

- *Team spirit*. Do I look for opportunities for building team-work into jobs?

- *Discipline*. Are the rules seen to be unreasonable? Am I fair and impartial in enforcing them?

- *Grievances*. Are grievances dealt with promptly? Do I take action on matters likely to disrupt the group?

- *Consultation*. Is this genuine? Do I encourage and welcome ideas and suggestions?

- *Briefing*. Is this regular? Does it cover current plans, progress and future developments?

- *Represent*. Am I prepared to represent and champion the feelings of the group when required?

- *Support*. Do I visit people at their work when the team is apart? Do I then represent, to the individual, the whole team in my manner and encouragement?

DEVELOPING THE INDIVIDUAL

- *Targets.* Have they been agreed and quantified?

- *Induction.* Does he or she really know the other team members and the organization?

- *Achievement.* Does he or she know how his or her work contributes to the overall result?

- *Responsibilities.* Is there a clear job description? Can I delegate more to him or her?

- *Authority.* Does he or she have sufficient authority to achieve his or her task?

- *Training.* Has adequate provision been made for training or retraining, both technical and as a team manager?

- *Recognition.* Do I emphasize people's success? In failure, is criticism constructive?

- *Growth.* Does he or she see a chance of development? Is there a career path?

- *Performance.* Is this regularly reviewed?

- *Reward.* Are work, capacity and pay in balance?

- *The task.* Is he or she in the right job? Has he or she the necessary resources?

- *The person.* Do I know this person well? What makes him or her different from others?

- *Time/attention.* Do I spend enough time with individuals in listening, developing and counselling?

- *Grievances.* Are these dealt with promptly?

- *Security.* Does he or she know about pensions, redundancy and so on?

- *Appraisal.* Is the overall performance of each individual regularly reviewed in face-to-face discussion?

FURTHER READING

To develop further your own leadership skills I suggest you read the following books that I have written:

Decision Making and Problem Solving Strategies (Kogan Page)

Effective Strategic Leadership (Pan Macmillan)

Not Bosses but Leaders (Kogan Page)

The Inspirational Leader (Kogan Page)

For key topics integral to leadership I recommend these titles in the Pan Macmillan series:

Effective Communication

Effective Decision-Making

Effective Innovation

Effective Motivation

Effective Teambuilding

Effective Time Management

Should you want to know more about what organizations can do to develop leaders, see my:

Effective Leadership Development (CIPD)

How to Grow Leaders (Kogan Page)

For full details of these books, together with training and self-development resources available from the Adair Leadership Foundation, visit www.johnadair.co.uk.

INDEX

Note: Page numbers in **bold** type denote **figures** and page numbers in *italic* type denote *tables*

Creating Success series

The above titles are available from all good bookshops.
For further information on these and other Kogan Page titles,
or to order online, visit the Kogan Page website at
www.koganpage.com